D0765157

MULTICULTURAL
LITERATURE

A READER'S GUIDE TO
AMY TAN'S

The Joy
Luck Club

PAMELA LOOS

Enslow Publishers, Inc.
40 Industrial Road
Box 398
Berkeley Heights, NJ 07922
USA
http://www.enslow.com

Library of Congress Cataloging-in-Publication Data

Loos, Pamela.
  A reader's guide to Amy Tan's The joy luck club / Pamela Loos.
    p. cm.—(Multicultural literature)
  Includes bibliographical references and index.
  Summary: "An introduction to Amy Tan's The Joy Luck Club for high school
students, which includes relevant biographical background on the author, explanations
of various literary devices and techniques, and literary criticism for the novice
reader"—Provided by publisher.
  ISBN–13: 978-0-7660-2832-6
  ISBN–10: 0-7660-2832-1
  1. Tan, Amy. Joy Luck Club—Juvenile literature. 2. Mothers and daughters in
literature. 3. Chinese Americans in literature. I. Title.
  PS3570.A48J635 2007
  813'.54—dc22
                              2006102440

Printed in the United States of America

10 9 8 7 6 5 4 3 2 1

Supports the English/Language Arts and Literature curricula.

To Our Readers: We have done our best to make sure all Internet addresses in this book were active and appropriate when we went to press. However, the author and the publisher have no control over and assume no liability for the material available on those Internet sites or on other Web sites they may link to. Any comments or suggestions can be sent by e-mail to comments@enslow.com or to the address on the back cover.

Illustration Credits: Amy Tierny/WireImage.com, p. 4; AP/ Wide World Photos, pp. 9, 15; Buena Vista Pictures, courtesy of the Everett Collection, Inc., pp. 71, 77; Everett Collection, Inc., pp. 21, 51; The Granger Collection, New York, p. 95 (top right); Rue des Archives/ The Granger Collection, New York, p. 95 (bottom left).

Cover Illustration: Kobal/ Buena Vista/ Hollywood/ The Kobal Collection/ WireImage.com.

Contents

Amy Tan

CHAPTER 1

Biography

"I said to myself when I was 17," Amy Tan, author of *The Joy Luck Club* recalled, "'I'm not going to have anything to do with anything Chinese when I leave home. I'm going to be completely American.' None of that Chinese torture or guilt ever again in my life. None of that responsibility... 'You owe it to your family. You have to do this for your family.' I was never going to speak to my mother again."[1]

But the teenager came to see things very differently years later, after a catastrophic event—her mother, Daisy, was hospitalized for a believed heart attack. That was when Amy Tan, already having lost a brother and her father, decided she needed to learn more about her mother and her mother's past. So much of that past had occurred in China, where her mother had been born and lived until 1949. Tan promised herself that if her mother pulled through, she would take her to visit China.

Tan's mother recovered, and in 1987 the mother and daughter set off on their trip. "So it [the trip] was a chance for me to really see what was inside of me and my mother," Tan told the Academy of Achievement in 1996. "Most importantly, I wanted to know about her past. I wanted to see where she had lived, I wanted to see the family members that had raised her, the daughters she had left behind. The daughters could have been me, or I could have been them."[2]

As Tan expected, the trip brought her many new insights. She realized how American she was, but she also realized how Chinese she was. That very side of her—Tan's Chinese heritage—that she had tried to ignore for so long suddenly did not seem so negative any more. Instead, Tan felt connected to China. She felt she was a part of its history. Whereas previously she had felt Chinese history was rather irrelevant, now she understood its importance and relevance.

Additionally, Tan saw her mother from a new perspective. Back in the United States, Tan had been embarrassed by her mother, who often appeared pushy, annoying, and insensitive. Frequently, Tan's mother would have confrontations with people. As a child, Tan had attributed these embarrassing confrontations to her mother's poor English and to cultural differences between the Chinese woman and Americans. Yet, in China, Tan saw that her mother remained not just her aggressive self but that she produced the same sort of reactions that she got in the United States.

Similarly, Tan observed her half sisters being distressed by their mother's comments—not only her comments to others, but to themselves. Daisy Tan made critical comments about her daughters' cooking and appearances, for instance.

Her daughters expected love, support, and warmth and instead, were upset to repeatedly experience something quite different. Still, Tan was reassured to see these reactions, which were similar to many she had felt toward her mother. Because of Tan's journey to China, she came to realize that her mother really did want the best for all of her daughters, even if she had an unconventional way of showing it.

Amy Tan was born on February 19, 1952, the second child of her mother, Daisy Tan, and father, John Tan. Her parents had very high expectations for their children. Early on, the two had decided that their daughter would be a neurosurgeon and concert pianist. Tan felt pressured not only by their expectations but also by warnings her mother would give her that were quite extreme and disturbing to a young person.

Daisy Tan strongly believed that her children should have a Chinese identity while exploring all the opportunities America offered. Daisy and her husband had come to the United States in the late

San Francisco's Chinatown displays signs in both English and Chinese, demonstrating the mixing of cultures. Growing up, Amy Tan struggled to reconcile her Chinese heritage with her American upbringing.

1940s and their friends were almost exclusively other Chinese immigrants. At Daisy Tan's urging, the family moved often. So, while Amy Tan was born in Oakland, California, she lived in several other cities in the San Francisco Bay area. As a result, she had to contend with the strains of adjusting each time the family moved. On top of this, she had to deal with feeling like she did not fit in because she was a Chinese American (there were no other Chinese Americans in most of her classes throughout high school).

Amy's feeling of not fitting in only intensified when both Amy's father and her older brother, Peter, died of brain tumors when Amy was a teenager. After this immense tragedy, Daisy Tan insisted on moving again, leaving California in 1968 and eventually settling with Amy and her younger brother, John, in Montreux, Switzerland.

Years later, Tan admitted that she fell apart after the family's tragic losses. Her reaction took the form of rebelling against her mother's conservativism. At age sixteen, Amy became involved with a twenty-four-year-old German man who had an illegitimate child. To Amy, at the time, the more that she could do to antagonize her mother, the better. When she was with the man's drug-dealing friends, Amy started drinking and smoking. After being arrested, Amy woke up and realized she had slipped too far. She broke off her relationship with the man and his friends and refocused her energies on school.

In 1969, Amy graduated from the Institut Monte Rosa Internationale, a high school in Montreux. Amy, her mother, and brother then returned to San Francisco. Amy started attending Linfield College, a small school in Oregon that her mother had chosen, believing its wholesome atmosphere would be good for her daughter. But again, Amy followed her own path. This time, after two semesters at Linfield, she switched schools. Amy transferred to San Jose City College in California in 1970 to be closer to her Italian-American boyfriend, Louis DeMattei. Daisy Tan was disturbed by this change and also by the fact that Amy changed her major from pre-med to a double major in English and linguistics. Amy's decisions were so distressing to Daisy that she and her daughter did not talk to each other for six months.

Amy Tan then transferred to San Jose State University and graduated with honors in 1972. She went on to earn a master's in linguistics from the same university in 1973. In 1974, she married

Louis DeMattei. Demattei had become a tax attorney and a man who, Tan said, was very kind and good, very much like her father. She started a doctoral program in linguistics at the University of California at Santa Cruz and later at the university's campus in Berkeley.

Tan's graduate studies were interrupted when one of her and Louis's close friends was brutally murdered. Tan decided to take time off from school so she could reevaluate her plans for the future. In 1976, she took a job as a language-development consultant with the Alameda County Association for Retarded Citizens. After that, for four years, Amy directed training programs for developmentally disabled children. She quit because she became fed up with being appointed to multiple governmental councils and task forces in order to be the voice for all minorities.

Tan then became a business writer. She had a partner, but when she later told him she wanted to do more writing, the partner disagreed and the two had a blowup. The partner said Tan could never make it on her own as a writer, but Tan became determined to prove him wrong. She soon became very successful, with major corporations for clients. She earned so much money that she bought Daisy Tan a house. Her mother was thrilled with Tan's success, but in time Tan became distressed, realizing she had turned into a workaholic. Tan began trying to change her life. She started by seeing a psychiatrist. When therapy did not help her, Tan turned to playing jazz piano, reading literature, and then to writing fiction and joining a writer's group. The group encouraged her fiction writing, and Tan worked on short stories. One of her published stories got the attention of an agent, Sandra Dijkstra, who agreed to represent Tan. While Tan was away with her mother in China in 1987, Dijkstra negotiated with a publisher for a book contract for Tan. Tan was so excited on learning the news that she folded her writing business and focused exclusively on writing her book, finishing it in just a few months.

Published in 1989, *The Joy Luck Club* was

well received. It was on the *New York Times* bestseller list for many months and was a finalist for the National Book Award for Fiction and the National Book Critics Circle Award.

After such great success, Tan was nervous about writing her next title and unsure even of what it should be about. After many false starts, she decided to stick with an account of her mother's life, told in a work of fiction, *The Kitchen God's Wife.* Even before its publication, publishers and book clubs were clamoring for various rights to the title, which appeared in 1991.

In 1992, Tan went on a different path, writing a children's book, *The Moon Lady.* She met yet another challenge when she decided to collaborate with screenwriter Ronald Bass to create a film version of *The Joy Luck Club.* The film was released in 1993, and by 1994 Tan published another children's title, *The Chinese Siamese Cat.*

By 1995 Tan published her next novel, *The Hundred Secret Senses*, which received mostly

On August 28, 1993, Amy Tan, actress Annette Benning, and director Wayne Wang attend the screening of the film version of *The Joy Luck Club.*

favorable reviews. It focused on many of the themes of her earlier titles, yet also delved into the supernatural and fantasy. Tan's next project was a novel about a daughter's grief over the death of her mother. When her own mother contracted Alzheimer's disease and died and her editor and friend died shortly thereafter, Tan knew the book, *The Bonesetter's Daughter*, needed more depth and rewrote it, publishing it in 2001.

In 2003, Tan took yet another route with her writing, publishing *The Opposite of Fate: A Book of Musings*, a collection of her own perspectives on life. Then, in 2005, in her book *Saving Fish from Drowning*, Tan abandoned her familiar topics concerning mother-daughter relationships and cultural and generational differences. Instead, she told the story of a group of vacationers. Some thought the book was funny and that it had engaging characters; others thought it silly at times and that its characters were stereotypes.

In addition to writing, Tan is part of the rock-and-roll band the Rock Bottom Remainders, comprised of famous authors, Stephen King, Scott Turow, and Matt Groening. The group performs across the United States and donates its money to charities. Tan and her husband have homes in San Francisco and New York.

CHAPTER 2

Narrative Style

While *The Joy Luck Club* is usually referred to as a novel, Tan has said she viewed the work as a collection of short stories. Indeed, the book is split into four sections, with each section, in turn, containing four stories. The themes and issues that are examined in these stories are related, and as the reader moves through the book, new information is revealed that ties later stories with earlier ones.

Each of the four sections starts with a tale. Most of these tales are metaphorical and all are told by an unknown narrator. In the first section and last section, each of three Chinese-American mothers tells a story; a fourth mother has recently died and so the fourth story in each of these two sections is told by her daughter. Sandwiched in between the first and last sections are two other sections, which also contain four stories each. These sections are told in the voices of the Chinese-American mothers' own daughters. In the various sections, the mothers and daughters closely examine their own lives as well as how they see each other. Their stories center on all the pain, pride, disappointment, and love that are inherent in mother-daughter relationships.

The first metaphorical tale is about a mother riding a swan to the United States to start a new life. There, she will have a daughter just like her, except for the fact that the daughter would not suffer the way the mother had throughout her own life. As the mother grows old, she is disturbed that she has never been able to tell her daughter about how she had the best intentions for her. Why? Because the mother wanted to tell her in perfect English rather than in her own halting speech. This tale sets the scene for the book and brings up issues that are addressed throughout—mothers wanting better lives for their daughters, having to go through a great deal to try to get these better lives, and not communicating about their pasts with their daughters.

The first story in this first section is told by Jing-mei, or June, Woo, whose mother, Suyuan Woo, has recently died. June meets with the women (who will also be narrators of stories in the book) and their husbands, who have been friends with Suyuan and her husband for years. These women surprise June by giving her money to visit her long-lost half sisters. Suyuan had finally found out where these daughters were. Only recently, and unfortunately after Suyuan's death, had they attempted to write her back. The mothers say June must meet the half sisters she has never known. She must tell them everything about their mother. June worries that she does not know her mother well enough to do so. The other mothers protest saying it is impossible for a daughter to not know her own mother.

The second story in this first section is told by An-Mei Hsu, whose mother had left her with her relatives. These relatives ingrained in the child that she must forget her mother because she disgraced the family. When An-Mei's mother returns, she sees her mother's love for her own mother.

The third story, told by Lindo Jong, is about her family marrying her off at a very young age to a husband who is cruel and who has a wicked and domineering mother. Lindo says that unlike her daughter, who does not worry about keeping promises, Lindo could not disgrace her family by leaving the marriage but found a way to trick the new family so that she could leave without disgrace.

The fourth story is told by Ying-ying St. Clair. She tells of being very young and part of a very wealthy family. She tells not of an enduring hardship, but about the fear she felt at a celebration where she lost her family. As in the other stories in this section, we see the emphasis on ties to the family. In this case we learn that the

The four mother-daughter pairs of the 1993 movie adaptation of *The Joy Luck Club*: (left to right) Kieu Chinh (Suyuan Woo); Ming-Na Wen (June Woo); Tamlyn Tomita (Waverly Jong); Tsai Chin (Lindo Jong); France Nuyen (Ying-ying St. Clair); Lauren Tom (Lena St. Clair); Lisa Lu (An-Mei Hsu); Rosalind Chao (Rose Hsu Jordan).

mother felt lost many times throughout her life and is concerned that her daughter is in the same unfortunate state. In this section, we see the common theme of abandonment and/or separation, and we learn some history about each of the mothers, told realistically and vividly from their own perspectives.

The second section begins with a story about a young girl who does not want to listen to her mother. The girl protests that her mother does not explain why she should listen to her warnings. The daughter finally refuses to listen, rushes off, and immediately gets hurt. All of the stories in this section tell of confrontations and/or differences between mothers and daughters. This section contains stories narrated by the daughters of the mothers who narrated the first section. In this section, just as in the first, the narrators are looking back into their childhoods.

In the first story, Waverly, the daughter of Lindo, recalls what it felt like being a young chess champion. Waverly is annoyed at how her mother brags about her chess skills. Waverly confronts her mother and the two end up not speaking to each other.

The second story is that of Lena. Lena is the daughter of Ying-ying, who, after her baby dies, has become a ghost of who she was. Ying-ying is basically absent from Lena's life and therefore the two are not fighting like some of the other characters. Even so, the narrative stays focused on confrontation and tension. In this case, the confrontation takes place between neighbors that the narrator overhears in terrible fights. Yet shortly after each fight, the neighbors sound happy.

The third story is that of Rose, daughter of An-Mei. Rose is afraid to tell her mother her marriage is heading for divorce. Rose recalls the horrific day that her brother drowned at the seashore and how her mother was determined to not believe he was truly dead. Back in the present, Rose thinks about how her mother will tell her to not give up on her marriage, even though Rose feels there is no hope.

The fourth story returns to a stronger confrontation between mother and daughter. In this story, June tells of how her mother tried to turn her into a pianist and how June fought her efforts. The fight becomes intense, and June strikes her mother's weak spot by saying she wishes she were dead like her half sisters. The comment shocks her mother into a silent retreat. The story ends with June, years later, sitting down at the piano and gaining a new perspective.

The third section starts with a story about a mother anticipating grandchildren and pointing out that they will be just like her daughter. The stories in this section are told by the daughters. They no longer focus on the past but mostly on their current relationship problems.

First Lena narrates, saying she is afraid of what her mother will see when it comes to her refurbished house and her problematic relation-ship with her husband. Indeed, her mother sees problems, and when her daughter says she knew something bad was going to happen, her mother asks why she did not do something about it.

Next, Waverly takes her mother to lunch. Yet she still cannot tell her she is getting married. When her mother and father finally have dinner with her boyfriend, it is a disaster. He inadver-tently insults the parents, and Waverly's mother has nothing good to say about him. When Waverly later confronts her mother about this, though, her mother appears different—defenseless almost. Waverly thinks about how she had run from her such a long time ago and kept a barrier between them for years.

In the third story, Rose feels better about her mother's advice about her crumbling marriage. She sees that her mother is on her side, encouraging her to stick up for herself. In the fourth story, too, a daughter sees her mother in a new light. June and her family have dinner with Waverly and her family. Waverly cruelly criticizes June and humiliates her in front of everyone. While cleaning up after the dinner, June sees herself differently and expects her mother to chastise her. Instead, she receives her mother's support.

The fourth section starts with a tale about a mother wanting the best for her daughter, but the mother is not sure she knows how to teach her daughter about life. The mother wants her daughter to lose her innocence but never lose hope and to always be able to laugh.

In this section, we return to the mothers as

narrators. We find out more about the mothers' difficult pasts during a war that devastated China. An-Mei witnesses the disgrace her mother endured and ultimately her mother's suicide. Ying-ying tells of how she married a man who left her and cheated on her. She aborted her own baby, became a lowly shopkeeper, and lost her spirit. In the third story, we learn that Lindo came to the United States on her own and how she made friends and found a husband. She realizes that her daughter needs to understand her mother's past. The book ends with June traveling to China with her father to meet her half sisters. She feels more in touch with the Chinese part of herself, and she finally learns the whole story of how her mother left her two daughters behind. June worries about the awkwardness of meeting her half sisters, and yet when they meet they are completely at ease and thrilled to see one another. June sees her mother in them.

CHAPTER 3

Themes

The Joy Luck Club focuses on relationships between immigrant mothers from China and their American-born daughters. The similarities in these relationships point to a number of recurring themes. One of the strongest of these is the message that despite great differences and misunderstandings (in this case between mothers and daughters, due to differences in culture and generations), all of us should appreciate our families and our heritages, and those who do so will be better for it. The novel shows repeated examples of daughters who do not understand their mothers and Chinese culture and are also embarrassed by them. At various times, the daughters are annoyed, frustrated, or intimidated by their mothers and so they dismiss the advice.

However, as the novel unfolds, we see, as the daughters do, that their mothers truly do know them and may not be so intimidating after all. Waverly, for instance, sees that she is the one who has created barriers between herself and her mother and that her mother is not such an overwhelming force. Lena, because of her mother, finally speaks up to her domineering husband and gives thought to her mother's simple question: Why not take preemptive action when you know something bad is waiting to happen? Rose is also surprised to find that her mother is not advising her to stay in an unhappy marriage but to speak up for herself.

Then there is June, the character who narrates the most in the novel. She is the one who, as a result of her mother dying, thinks about her mother and their relationship the most as well. She also examines what it means to her to be of Chinese descent. She, like the other daughters, sees where her mother has been right (her mother always said June would start but not finish things). Because of her mother's death June visits China to meet her half sisters. June then recognizes the importance of embracing one's heritage. No other daughter in the novel makes a trip to China, although Waverly plans to do so with her husband and thinks it might not even be so bad to go with her mother as well.

The novel also shows that while the daughters may be looking for a clearly definable Chinese culture, few if any cultures are clearly definable. As one critic noted,

> *Tan also invokes a stereotypical emblem of Americanness in the materialistic and modern cultural icon, Coca-Cola. Yet, like the symbol of the swan, this sign is already unstable and dislocated from its supposed referent. For, while Coca-Cola has come to represent "Americanness," in fact, in this period of*

SYMBOL
Something that stands for, represents, or suggests another thing.

late-capitalism the corporation of Coca-Cola is found throughout the world. The transnational character of this icon registers the economic and cultural imperialism entailed in the success of Americanization on a global scale, while contradicting its status as American; for, it both is and is not American. This instability continuously interrogates what it means to be "American."[1]

The mothers want their daughters to get the most they can from an American life. However, the mothers frequently show their misunderstandings and prejudices about Americans, just as Americans show theirs about the Chinese. The mothers also remain, to a great degree, in their own world. They do not absorb American culture and speak only fractured American English or Chinese. The daughters in the novel, however, learn American ways and all speak English well. One critic comments on the differences:

Mastering this imaginary perfect English for the American-born daughter turns out not to be a simple ticket to

American success. This linguistic competency, ironically,

signifies her departure from her mother (and her

motherland), deepening the chasm between generations

and cultures. Moreover, learning to speak perfect

American English may also entail the complex journey of

"successful" acculturation which often masks the racism

and sexism that belie the American dream.[2]

One of the most disturbing examples of an American's racism
in the novel is that of
Rose Hsu Jordan's
mother-in-law. Early
in Rose's relationship
with Ted, before she
marries him, Rose meets
Ted's mother, Mrs. Jordan. The
woman purposefully takes Rose aside to talk with
her. She tells her that she and her husband "per-
sonally knew many fine people who were
Oriental, Spanish, and even black."[3] However,
since Ted would be becoming a doctor, they would

IRONY
The incongruity of an expected
situation and the actual situation.
In language, irony is the deliberate use of words to contrast an
apparent meaning with the words'
intended meaning (which are usually the complete opposite of
each other).

be in situations where others might not accept minorities as the Jordans do. She also tells Rose that other people are not as accepting of minorities in light of the Vietnam War. Mrs. Jordan mistakenly assumes Rose is Vietnamese. While trying to blame prejudice on others only, she shows her own prejudice against Rose and other minorities.

The daughters in the novel also see prejudice in their own mothers when it comes to their daughters' relationships with American men. Rose's mother warns Rose that her boyfriend is American, as if this alone should make him undesirable. Rose responds that she is American, too. Waverly also sees her own mother being unhappy about Waverly's plan to marry an American. These situations point to the difficulties of being a second-generation Chinese American.

Several other instances of prejudice appear in the novel. These and the earlier examples show that just like the gap between mothers and daughters, a gap between cultures leads to confusion, pain, and missed opportunities for enrichment. In a more minor example of cultural differences in the novel, a Caucasian man asks a young Waverly and her friends if he can take their picture in front of a Chinese restaurant. He purposefully has them stand so that the picture can include the hanging roasted duck in the restaurant window, an image foreign to many Americans.

Even at her young age, Waverly sees the man as out of his element in this section of town. No tourists even go to this restaurant, where the menu is only printed in Chinese. Waverly shows her mischievous side when she tells the man with the camera that he should eat in the restaurant. When he innocently asks what they serve, she shouts, "Guts and duck's feet and octopus gizzards!"[4] She wants to further the distance between the Chinese and this man. Waverly knows, too, how Americans can hold their own negative assumptions about Chinese food; she plays on what she assumes will be the man's prejudices.

In another example of people making

unwarranted and prejudiced assumptions about other cultures, people see Lena (whose father is not Chinese and so she does not have a strong Chinese appearance) with her mother Ying-ying and assume that Ying-ying is Lena's maid. Not only do the people not realize that Lena could be Ying-ying's daughter, but they also assume that the older woman, who definitely appears Chinese, must have an unskilled job, subservient to the woman with her that they probably believe is purely Caucasian.

Aside from addressing the harmful effects of prejudices across cultures, the novel also comments on the horrors of prejudices against women. In one such example, An-mei looks back on being a little girl and describes her family and others celebrating the Moon Festival, which focuses on the story of the Moon Lady, who on this special day fulfills secret wishes. Usually, An-mei's servant reminds her, girls are not to think of their own needs and are never to ask for anything but are only to listen. Later, when An-mei sees someone depicting the part of the Moon Lady, the Moon Lady cries out some of the believed differences between men and women, "For woman is yin, . . . the darkness within, where untempered passions lie. And man is yang, bright truth lighting our minds."[5]

Yet the prejudices do not appear only in Chinese stories; rather, they are an accepted part of Chinese society at the time when the mothers in the novel are younger. At this time, once a woman in China is a widow, there are almost no options for her. This is why An-mei's mother becomes the fourth wife (though the others are all still living and considered wives as well) to a wealthy man. Eventually, An-Mei's mother kills herself because of her desperate situation. Similarly, we see that Suyuan and Ying-ying must wait to hear that their husbands are dead before they can remarry.

We see also that there is great emphasis in the Chinese culture on having sons. When the Joy Luck Club meets in China, for instance, the women eat boiled peanuts. They believe these will help them conceive sons. Also, even though concubines are seen as a disgraced part of society, they are even worse off if they cannot produce a son.

The unfairness of how women are treated is also apparent in the fact that while concubines are disgraced, the men who have them are not. Additionally, a woman's overall standing is dependent on her husband. When the novel opens, a narrator talks of how she wants to leave this concept behind. In her vision, in the United States "nobody will say her worth is measured by the loudness of her husband's belch."[6]

Aside from themes about the damaging effects of prejudice, the novel has a theme that declares the importance of making the best of one's situation. The novel's title takes the name of the club that Suyuan formed to take the women's minds off the hardships they endured in war-torn China. When the women immigrate to America, the club lives on, indicating that no matter what happens, one should not look back with regret but should look forward with hope. All of the mothers reflect on painful incidents from their pasts, yet all were strong enough to move to a new country and idealistic enough to believe they would have better lives.

At times this idealism too strongly blocks the past. We see that all of the mothers have kept their pasts a secret from their daughters (although Suyuan does reveal much about her past to June). We also see the ramifications of this. Part of the reason the daughters do not understand their mothers and their Chinese culture is because secrets are being kept. There is a theme, then, that secrets are harmful. By the end of the novel, the mothers realize the importance of truly sharing their pasts with their daughters.

CHAPTER 4

Literary Devices

As mentioned earlier, *The Joy Luck Club* is composed of a series of sixteen interlocking stories, told by different narrators, each of whom is part of a mother-daughter pair. What is interesting about how the stories are told is not only how the characters' perspectives change, but also how our own perspective about the characters changes as the book progresses.

For instance, early in the book we are told June's story about visiting the women of the Joy Luck Club. They can be tough, pushy, and unfeeling—yet at the same time they are quite generous, especially when they give June the money to visit her half sisters. In this story we also learn about June's mother and see that she shares some of the same negative traits as the women in the club. The remaining stories in the first section tell some of the heartache these mothers withstood in their own pasts.

By the second section of the book, however, we see more of the flaws of the mothers and, to some degree, of the daughters. We see, for instance, how Suyuan and Lindo push their daughters and annoy them by interfering in their lives. We also see how abandoned Lena feels when her mother becomes basically helpless after the trauma of losing her baby. And we see how Rose is made to witness her mother's excessively desperate attempts to find her son who is drowned, believing her own faith can bring him back to life. In Rose's story in this section (and in the other stories throughout the book), we see the powerful role of superstition in these mothers' lives and how that superstition disturbs the families. As much as we see negative consequences of the mothers' personalities, though, in two of the daughters' stories in this section we also see how manipulative and cruel some of the daughters can be to their mothers.

By the third section, we see more of the daughters' flaws. We see how all of them have had trouble in their personal relationships. In the case of June, we see how she has had a negative relationship with Waverly. We see that the mothers may be right for feeling that they should step in and try to help their daughters. We also begin to see how the mothers really do know their daughters, even though the daughters do not know their mothers— again giving us a more positive perspective on the mothers.

In the fourth section, we learn more about the difficulties in the mothers' pasts and gain more respect for them. By the time we get to this section, we are seeing both mothers and daughters as more complex and human. Mothers are admitting that while they have tried their best, they have made mistakes. Daughters are seeing that their mothers are not so bad after all. In the case of

June, who tells the most stories (since she also narrates for her dead mother), we even see a daughter realize the importance of learning more about her mother and her Chinese roots.

Tan has transformed not only her characters but also our perceptions of these characters as well. She seems to be warning us not to jump to quick conclusions. Additionally, we realize that those living a modern life should see the value and wisdom of earlier generations and their culture. As one critic put it, Tan "demonstrates how many intertwined dilemmas can impede or frustrate clear access by daughters to their mothers and to the full stories of their mother's and family's life and history in China and America. Nevertheless, Tan's text emphasizes that this difficult work of recovery is vital to women's well-being and solidarity with each other."[1]

Aside from focusing on changing characters and our perceptions of them, Tan pays great attention to how each character tells her stories. Vivid imagery, for example, is frequent, giving us

a clearer vision of the storytellers and their experiences. As one critic noted, "*The Joy Luck Club*
is repeatedly applauded by reviewers for the speci-
ficity of its descriptions—entire 'richly textured
worlds' evoked by details 'each . . . more haunting
and unforgettable than the one before.' The book
is called 'dazzling because of the worlds it gives
us'; the word 'tapestry' is used to describe this
effect of intricacy and richness.'"[2]

In the beginning of the book, for instance,
Suyuan describes in vivid detail Kweilin, a place in
China that is more beautiful than she ever imagined:

> *The peaks looked like giant fried fish heads trying to jump*
> *out of a vat of oil. . . . And then the clouds would move*
> *just a little and the hills would suddenly become monstrous*
> *elephants marching slowly toward me! . . . Inside [the*
> *caves] grew hanging rock gardens in the shapes and colors*
> *of cabbage, winter melons, turnips, and onions. These*
> *were things so strange and beautiful you can't ever*
> *imagine them.*[3]

But, as mentioned, Tan does not only use imagery to give us a detailed mental vision of a foreign place. She also puts imagery to use to grab her readers in other ways. In a horrific and ironic case, Tan describes how Chinese newspapers lay scattered in the streets proclaiming Kweilin safe from the Japanese army, but on top of these very newspapers lay many dead Chinese, lined up "like fresh fish from a butcher."[4]

Tan also uses imagery to provide a clearer understanding of characters and how they think. When Waverly thinks back to when she was a chess champion, for example, she remembers how she tried to devise a strategy for winning the battle of wills with her mother. She saw her mother as her chess opponent and envisioned herself and her mother at a chessboard, with her mother's pieces ominously advancing and her own pieces crying out as they fell from the board. Tan creatively brings us into the mind of a young girl who spends so much time strategizing about her chess games that she comes to imagine life as a chess game as well.

Aside from using imagery to keep her readers involved, Tan uses metaphorical stories. As mentioned earlier, each of the four sections of *The Joy Luck Club* starts with a story told by an unknown narrator. Most of these have a fairy tale-like quality and also contain imagery as well as metaphors. The reader is not told these stories' meanings directly, then, but is made to think about them.

Tan also frequently has the mothers in her book tell their daughters metaphorical stories. Here we assume the belief is that a child will be more likely to remember a story and its consequences than the child would remember a single sentence of advice. What happens, though, is that the children do not realize that the tales they are told are metaphors and are not to be taken literally. As a result, they become overly frightened when they hear stories—about a little girl who does not listen to her mother and therefore sees her brain fall out of her ear or about a little girl who is so greedy that her stomach grows huge and a whole melon is inside.

Tan also uses the technique of suspense in her work. Most notably, Suyuan keeps telling her daughter the story of how she left her home because of the war between China and Japan. June has heard the story many times and believes it to be fiction since the ending keeps changing. It is a gripping story even as fiction, but then June finally hears a new ending and realizes the story is true: Her mother was married to someone before she was married to June's father, and her mother left her two daughters from that marriage in China, not knowing if they would be saved or killed. Near the beginning of *The Joy Luck Club* we also learn that the two daughters have written to Suyuan. However, it is only in the very last story of the book that we learn how Suyuan left her daughters, who had taken care of them, and how Suyuan had continued to search for them.

Tan uses suspense in other ways as well. While her book contains sixteen stories, most of which can be read as independent short stories, there are some that leave us wondering what happened next. In *The Joy Luck Club*, what did happen next might not be found out until a certain character becomes narrator again later in the text.

On a smaller scale, Tan also builds suspense by giving ominous warnings. For example, when a matchmaker looks for a marriage partner for a young male baby, we know the boy's marriage will be bad because of the negative traits that are already apparent in the baby boy. The reader wonders what dreadful things will happen. In other cases, Tan is even more direct in using suspense. For example, we know that something intriguing has happened when a character says that she knows what *really* happened. By having a character say this, Tan gets the reader to start wondering what did ultimately happen.

CHAPTER 5

Suyuan Woo and Jing-mei "June" Woo

Suyuan Woo, the originator of the Joy Luck Club, died at age seventy-one, shortly before the main plot of the novel takes place. She was married to Canning Woo, age seventy-two, who worked at a newspaper in China; the two moved to the United States together many years before. June is Suyuan and Canning's daughter and was born in the United States. Suyuan has two other daughters from a previous husband; they were born in China.

Like the other women in the group, Suyuan was annoying, pushy, and strong. Her daughter sees her as having been perpetually displeased with others, even her own family, and openly critical of them. In China, Suyuan was married to an army officer and had two daughters with him. With her husband away, she depended on herself to remain strong and hopeful, even though the Japanese were bombing and invading China. In the midst of this chaos, she formed the Joy Luck Club, a sign of her determination to remain hopeful for good luck in the future. Suyuan invited three other women into the club, and the foursome met once a week to play mahjong, eat, win some money, and tell stories to boost each others' spirits, despite the terror around them. When Suyuan moved to the United States, she saw other Chinese immigrants trying to adjust to their new lives; she invited three of them and their spouses to start a U.S. version of the club.

Like the other mothers in the club, Suyuan wanted the best for her daughter, June. She idealistically believed that in America, people can become whatever they want to be and achieve amazing success. Suyuan believed she could find hidden talents in her daughter and tried to have her follow in the footsteps of other child prodigies she read about or saw on television.

Also like the other mothers, Suyuan tried to teach her daughter how to think (as Suyuan sees it) like a Chinese person. Yet, like the other daughters in the novel, June is more intrigued with American ways than with learning Chinese ways. Part of the reason that Chinese ways are pushed into the background by June and the other daughters in the novel is that the mother-daughter pairs often have difficulty understanding each other. Even when June is trying to listen, she often does not understand the point of her mother's stories and comments. One commentator remarks on the communication issues and their consequences:

> The mothers' inability to speak perfect American English has multiple ramifications. For one thing, as they themselves have not lived in a foreign country, the daughters are left with the false impression that their mothers are not intelligent. As a result, the daughters often feel justified in believing that their mothers have nothing worthwhile to say. Furthermore, when mother and daughter share neither

the same realm of experience and knowledge nor the same

concerns, their differences are not marked by a slip of the

tongue or the lack of linguistic adroitness or even by a gen-

erational gap, but rather by a deep geographical and

cultural cleft.[1]

Suyuan stands out from the other mothers, not only because she formed the Joy Luck Club, but also because she did tell her daughter some stories about her past in China. While at first her daughter did not realize the stories were true, they became clear. After Suyuan retold her story over and over, she finally gave the real ending: Suyuan left two of her daughters in China while fleeing the Japanese army invasion. Suyuan took the bold step of sharing a very painful time with her daughter and was also willing to admit to doing something that many might not understand. She abandoned her daughters because she had traveled so far and could not make it another step.

One critic points out the value of storytelling in this way: "Both Tan and Kingston allow their

An exhausted Suyuan Woo struggles to escape the Japanese army with her daughters in the film adaptation of *The Joy Luck Club.*

female characters to reclaim and recreate their identity. 'Storytelling heals past experiences of loss and separation; it is also a medium for rewriting stories of oppression and victimization into parables of self-affirmation and individual empowerment.'"[2]

June is thirty-six years old, and a copywriter at a small advertising agency. After her mother dies, her father asks her to take her mother's place at the Joy Luck Club meetings.

Like the other daughters in the novel, June

has had differences with her mother. Like Waverly, as a young girl June had a heated fight with her mother because she felt her mother's pride in her needed to be diminished. While Waverly had a natural talent for chess, Suyuan tried to find a great talent in June but did not succeed. At age nine, June was initially excited about finding something she was talented at:

> In all of my imaginings, I was filled with a sense that I would soon become perfect. My mother and father would adore me. I would be beyond reproach. I would never feel the need to sulk for anything.
>
> But sometimes the prodigy in me became impatient. "If you don't hurry up and get me out of here, I'm disappearing for good," it warned. "And then you'll always be nothing."[3]

The quote shows that June had a poor image of herself, seeing herself as "nothing." Also, it shows that she felt that her parents' love for her was dependent on how successful she was. As Suyuan made more and more attempts to find

June's skill and none of the attempts worked, June's insecurities about herself became even stronger. Distressed when she saw how many different things she could not do well, June decided that she just would not try.

We see just how stubborn she was when she took piano lessons. By a twist of fate, her piano teacher was deaf, so she got away with going for numerous lessons, continually doing poorly. She was so determined to not do well that she did not concern herself with practicing for an upcoming concert where she would be performing. Curiously, when June got on stage, she was excited about being there, but by the time her performance was over she was mortified over how many mistakes she made and at the embarrassment she caused herself and her family.

After June's great failure on stage, she was shocked that her mother still wanted her to take piano lessons and the two got into a yelling match. We see that June was willing to be quite hurtful to her mother. First, June told her mother she wished she were not her daughter. Then when that did not stop her mother, she said she wished she were dead, like the daughters her mother had left in China. Of course, the young June did not know what had happened to her half sisters left in China, but the words were so shocking that her mother was left speechless and never made June take piano lessons again.

Of all the daughters in the novel, June is the one that, after her mother's death, searches for answers to questions about her mother and about what it means to be Chinese. She is forced to take her mother's place at the mahjong table and also to be her representative when visiting her half sisters in China. By having lost her mother, she actually does get to know more about her and about China. Also, presumably, as she continues to attend the club meetings, she will learn more from the others about her mother and about being Chinese. Since the mothers give her money to meet her half sisters, she thinks about what she will tell her half sisters about their mother. The visit, in turn, will get her to learn more about China and their lives, an extension of her mother.

June recognizes some things about her relationship with her mother as well. For instance, she used to dismiss her mother's criticism of her for not finishing things, such as not graduating from college. Now she sees the validity of such criticism.

CHAPTER 6

Lindo Jong and Waverly Jong

Lindo has immigrated to the United States from China. She is the wife of Tin Jong, also a Chinese immigrant, and the mother of Waverly and two sons, all of whom were born in the United States. She is in her sixties or seventies, like the other women in the Joy Luck Club. Lindo, like the others, has remained a part of the group since its inception. Suyuan Woo is said to have been Lindo's best friend but also her enemy since the two constantly compared their daughters, each trying to prove her daughter was the best.

Lindo's past proves how important she believes it is to be loyal to one's family. At a young age, she was married off by her family even though she did not want to go with the new husband and his family. Lindo felt strongly that she should not disgrace her family by leaving the marriage, however, even when she saw how cruel the new husband and his mother were to her. Years later, she is distressed that her own daughter does not realize the importance of promises and readily breaks them.

Lindo is also keen enough to realize that Chinese ways are not always the best. For instance, when she is forced into an unhappy marriage, she does not blame her family, but society and the archaic way of thinking that existed out in the Chinese countryside. She rejects matchmaking. Also, when her family loses their home due to a massive flood, she comments on how there was no insurance company to help them. Again, she sees advantages in modernity and life in the United States.

At the same time, Lindo can see one of her big mistakes when it came to her vision of bringing up her daughter. She had thought it possible to teach her daughter Chinese beliefs while at the same time letting her daughter take advantage of all the United States had to offer. Lindo realizes that while she had the best of intentions, her plan did not work. She is willing to confront her mistake.

Lindo is also sharp enough to realize that it can be harmful to pretend one is happy when one is not. When she did this in her marriage, she later realizes, she was living a delusional life. She was like many American housewives who convince themselves they are happy to stay at home and focus on small, mundane tasks. Lindo empathizes with American women who had also been made submissive.

We learn that Lindo is smart and tricky. While she is still young and in the early years of her marriage, she develops a scheme for getting out of her arranged marriage without disgracing her family. She is shrewd and observant enough to manipulate her husband, his family, and the matchmaker, using their superstitious natures against them.

We also see that Lindo is strong and determined. Even as a baby, she pushes the matchmaker
away. Later, when married and controlled by her
horrid mother-in-law and husband, she realizes,
even before she plans her escape from the unhappy marriage, that she will always be herself and
that no one can change that. Once free of her
husband, she makes further plans to improve
her life. She pays a woman to help prepare her for
moving to America. She makes the journey and,
once there, she finds a job and a new husband.

Lindo also makes comments to people that
are hurtful, and it is not always clear whether she
realizes how the comments affect others. Most
distressing for Lindo's daughter, Waverly, is the
way Lindo reacts to her daughter's new American
boyfriend. Lindo does what she can to refrain
from talking about him, but when her daughter
forces her to say something about him, she has
only negative remarks. In one commentary on the
novel, a critic was quoted: "the object of 'confrontation' for a daughter is often the mother,

'the source of authority for her and the most single powerful influence from China.'"[1]

Waverly is in her thirties, a tax attorney at Price Waterhouse. She was married to Marvin, with whom she had a daughter, Shoshana, who is four years old. While Waverly is intimidated by her mother, she is not intimidated by others. Her friend remarks on how Waverly can stand up to the IRS, for instance. Like her mother, Waverly makes unfeeling remarks to others. As a young girl, after Waverly witnesses June's very poor piano performance on stage, she tells June that June will never be a genius like she is. Similarly, as a dinner guest at the Woo's home, Waverly is the first to choose a crab for her daughter, future husband, and herself, and she chooses the best for each, without regard to what is left for the others.

At the same dinner, Waverly is cruel to June in front of everyone. While she compliments June's haircut, she says June should go to Waverly's stylist instead. Although, she adds, June probably could not afford it. As with Lindo, it is unclear if Waverly realizes how her comments affect others or if she cares. June fights back by saying maybe she could afford such a haircut if Waverly's company paid her for her work. Waverly tells June that the work was unacceptable. She says she tried to get people at the company to see it differently but this did not work. Here, Waverly's trying to help, makes her seem like she cares. However, this impression is lost when Waverly makes fun of what June has written and has everyone at the dinner table laughing at June's work. Curiously, it is Lindo who comes to June's defense.

Further examination of Waverly reveals other ways that she is similar to her mother. She, like her mother, sees how women are ill treated in society. She asks why the chess set has no women and children. She sees the merit in being a prodigy who is also female, and she notes Bobby Fischer's sexist comment that a woman would never achieve grand-master status.

Waverly acknowledges that her mother's

Waverly Jong's perspective of her mother Lindo changes over the course of the story. Waverly recognizes the part she played in straining the relationship between them and comes to better understand her mother.

teachings have helped her, in life overall as well as in chess. She has taught her, for instance, to hold her tongue, to not let out her secrets or strengths.

At the same time, however, the daughter learns that the same strategies can be used against her. When she lashes out at her mother, letting her know how angry she is about how her mother brags about the chess winnings, the daughter sees the confrontation as an intense game of wits. Yet, as one critic explained, Waverly "herself is finally a victim of her mother's more authoritarian deployment of the tactic [of keeping quiet], as it suddenly takes the form of simply ignoring her."[2]

As an adult, Waverly recalls the confrontation with her mother, how she did not understand her mother's critical reaction when Waverly finally gave in, started talking to her mother again, and said she would play chess again. As an adult, she realizes she still has some of the same feelings toward her mother that she did then. Now, again, she is angry, hurt, and not able to understand her mother. This time it is because her mother does not want to talk about her boyfriend Rich and her mother says only negative things about him when she finally does. When the daughter confronts her mother about how she feels, she is confused by her mother's reaction but then sees her in a new light. Waverly sees her mother as a woman who is not as fierce as she imagined and who has been barricaded from her daughter because her own daughter has set up the barricade.

CHAPTER 7

Ying-ying St. Clair and Lena St. Clair

Ying-ying was born in China and is the wife of Clifford St. Clair, an English-Irish American whom she met in China. The two moved to the United States where they had their daughter, Lena. Clifford died about a year before the main story of *The Joy Luck Club* takes place.

Ying-ying stands out among the women in the club for often seeming to be consumed by her thoughts and daydreams. Like the other mothers, she is superstitious. She wants her daughter to be the best, believes in Chinese ways, and has had a troubled past. Although she has come from a very rich Chinese family, that wealth had its own drawbacks and could not save her from Chinese custom. She is the woman in the group who appears to have been the most harmed by her past.

As a young child, Ying-ying spent most of her time with her servant but longed for more time with her mother. She was wild, stubborn, vain, and would not listen. She suffered a trauma at the age of four when she fell off the large boat on which her family was celebrating. No one on the boat noticed, but luckily she got picked up by people fishing. As one essayist described it:

> [T]hey attempt to restore her to her family group by hailing a floating pavilion to tell those aboard they have found the lost child. Instead of the family appearing to reclaim her, Ying-ying sees only strangers and a little girl who shouts, "That's not me. . . . I'm here. I didn't fall in the water."
>
> What seems a bizarre, comically irrelevant mistake is the most revealing and shocking moment of the story, for it is as if her conscious self has suddenly appeared to deny her, to cast her permanently adrift in a life among strangers.[1]

Indeed, Ying-ying repeatedly says she is lost at various points in the narrative and fears that her daughter is in the same predicament. In China, Ying-ying was married to a man who cheated on her, impregnated her, and abandoned her. She aborted the child and went to live with poor cousins, and eventually became a lowly shop girl. Only after her husband died was she free to marry Clifford.

Whereas a repeated theme in *The Joy Luck Club* is about making the best of things, Ying-ying is unable to do so for many years. When Lena was a young girl, Ying-ying again became pregnant. Her superstitions and belief that something was wrong overpowered her. When she lost the baby, she had a breakdown, wildly recalling the earlier baby she had destroyed.

Like most of the other mothers in the text, Ying-ying does come to some realizations that we assume will transform her relationship with her daughter. When she stays at her daughter's house, she vows that her daughter, who has continuously been distancing herself from her mother, must be saved from her bad life. She decides that the best way to help is to tell her daughter her whole life story, so she will know who her mother really is.

Ying-ying sees her daughter as having no chi, or life force. As one observer explained, "The chi that she refers to may be impossible to render wholly into English, but it involves a fundamental self-respect, a desire to excel, a willingness to stand up for one's self and one's family, to demonstrate something to others. It may well be a quality that the daughters in the book lack, or that they possess in insufficient amounts."[2]

Lena is thirty-four years old and married to Harold Livotny. He is a partner at Livotny & Associates, an architectural firm, and she is an associate there.

At a young age, Lena felt the fearfulness and anxiety that her mother also felt. She hoped life would improve when the family moved into a new apartment. However, just the opposite happened. Her mother's anxiety increased because she felt things were out of balance and out of harmony. Lena learned that her mother was pregnant. This, too, disturbed her mother, who kept bumping into things and speaking of a heaviness.

Lena did not understand how her father did not feel the things that she and her mother did and how he never worried. While he appeared to be an agreeable, kind person, he only knew a few Chinese phrases and insisted that his wife speak only in English. Ying-ying did not know much English, and Lena frequently translated things for her. Lena knows English and Chinese rather well. As a result, she has the biggest advantage in the family when it comes to communication. She admits that she has translated things differently to her mother when it would work to Lena's advantage. She would do this when she was embarrassed by something her mother had said or done. Being a translator also had its burdens, though. When Lena's mother lost her baby and began to fall apart, Lena did not translate for her father exactly what her mother said. She was concerned her mother was crazy and did not want to let her father know this.

This event marked the beginning of Ying-ying's breakdown. Lena saw it happen a step at a time and was nervous. Her father, too, started to fall apart, making Lena more anxious. Even at a young age, though, Lena gained a more positive perspective.

Lena had been seriously disturbed by sounds she heard through her bedroom wall at night. She heard her neighbors, a mother and daughter, fighting ferociously. The fighting took on new significance one night when the girl appeared at the St. Clairs' doorstep. She told Lena she was going to trick her mother, who thought the girl was locked out of their apartment. She would climb through Lena's window and go across the fire escape and back to her own bedroom. In the meantime, her mother would be worried about her daughter being locked out. Lena watched the girl climb out the window and later heard the girl and her mother begin yelling but then laughing and sounding happy.

Ying-ying St. Clair shows concern over her daughter Lena's unhappiness in her marriage in the film adaptation of *The Joy Luck Club*.

Ten-year-old Lena was shocked at the happy exchange. From this she came to a new conclusion: Even though her mother seemed a ghost of herself, this was the worst and that life would get better. However, Ying-ying did get better, Lena later became anorexic.

Later, when Lena is married and her mother visits, Lena worries about what her mother will see while staying in Lena and Harold's home. In fact, her mother does find a list on the refrigerator that shows the expenses, even very small ones, that Lena has paid for and that Harold has paid for. The list has already been antagonizing Lena. Harold and she are nitpicking rather than operating as a couple.

Later, when Harold and Lena are alone, Lena lets Harold know things are bothering her. Her mother seems to have pushed her to a realization that things should be better. That same evening, Lena tells her mother she knew something bad was going to happen. Ying-ying asks her why she did not do something about it. In this exchange we see that Ying-ying has caused the disturbance Lena anticipated, but that it can produce positive results.

CHAPTER 8

An-mei Hsu and Rose Hsu Jordan

An-mei Hsu is another member of the Joy Luck Club. She is married to George Hsu, who is a pharmacist's assistant and had been a doctor in China. The couple had four sons and three daughters. Rose is the middle child.

As with the other mothers in the novel, early in the text we get a small taste of An-mei's personality. For instance, An-mei had gone to China to visit her relatives, only to have them take advantage of her generosity. An-mei is not so quick to brag as some of the others. For example, she willingly admits Suyuan is the best mahjong player in their group.

Of all the mothers' stories, An-mei's stories in *The Joy Luck Club* involve her own mother and grandmother to the greatest degree. Early on, she felt intensely abandoned by her mother and suffered greatly because of this. Her stories tell the pain of an intense divide within her family. They also point to the horrors of Chinese custom, as other stories in the novel have. For not only was An-mei left by her mother at a very young age, but she was also left with relatives who were cruel to her and who could not forgive her mother for becoming a concubine. Only later do we learn that An-mei's mother, who had been married to a scholar and became a widow, was raped. As a result, she had few options open to her in Chinese society.

Aside from feeling abandoned, as a young child An-mei suffered harshness from her aunt, uncle, and grandmother, whom she and her brother lived with. Whereas her brother was willing to rebel against the relatives and at times enjoy himself, this did not seem to be An-mei's disposition. In some of the earlier stories in the novel, we see that the young An-mei was often frightened as a child. She, like others, took metaphorical tales literally, believing that her brain could actually fall out of her head if she protested and shook it too much; that her stomach could grow to an enormous size if she did not refrain from greediness; that her father, although dead, still could see every bad thing she did since the eyes in his portrait were watching her.

An-mei clearly remembers her mother leaving and wanting to bring An-mei with her. An-mei tried to go toward her mother, but the young girl was seriously burned by blisteringly hot soup. She suffered greatly burns. Her grandmother told her that she was close to death and might forever be forgotten by her mother. Although An-mei was horribly frightened by such a possibility, she recovered. Later, An-mei showed her courage and intense need for her mother when her mother returned and asked her if she wanted to come and live with her. The young girl left with her mother despite the great protest of her other relatives. She really knew nothing of what her life would be like other than that she would be disgraced forever because of the choice.

Much later in life we see An-mei as a person of desperate hope. When her son fell into the waves and disappeared, she refused to give up searching for him. Perhaps because she remembers the agony of being abandoned by her own mother, once An-mei is a mother herself, believes she can protect her children despite her superstitions that they are vulnerable to great disaster. After her son's death, we see that she has written his name in the family bible's death list in erasable pencil.

Years later, An-mei is perceptive enough to see that her daughter's husband is cheating on her. She is also perceptive enough to see that the psychiatrist is not helping her daughter. She tells her daughter that a mother knows more about her daughter than a psychiatrist. She realizes that even the lowly peasant can rise up against strong forces and win. An-mei hopes her daughter can do the same.

Rose, who is in her thirties, works as a

production assistant for graphic artists, and is married to Ted, a dermatologist. Rose is afraid to tell her mother that she is getting a divorce. She knows her mother will tell her not to give up on her marriage, and Rose does not want to hear that. Rose remembers her mother's determination to fight on the day that her little brother fell into the waves and was never found. She vividly recalls

An-Mei Hsu and Rose Hsu Jordan share a moment of understanding in the film adaptation of *The Joy Luck Club.*

how her mother refused to give up on finding him alive, even after the emergency workers realized the body was not to be found, and told the family to go home.

Rose looks back on her marriage and sees its flaws. She did have a rebellious spirit, because Ted was there for her to lean on. Ted was American which caused troubles with the couple's families. Rose realizes she picked Ted because he was so different from the Chinese partners her siblings had found. She, like the other daughters in the novel, is not content with following traditional Chinese ways. Yet, when Ted's mother draws Rose aside and reveals her prejudices and that she thinks it is a mistake for Rose and Ted to be together, Ted says they cannot give in. Rose is ready to fight and stay in the relationship. She imagines herself as victim and Ted as her hero, always saving her.

Once the two are married, Ted makes all the decisions. Later, after he makes a serious mistake with a patient, he pushes Rose to make some decisions. She has a very tough time making any decisions and the relationship is strained. Rose realizes that you cannot depend on others to save you, just as no one was able to save her younger brother.

As a little girl, Rose remembers her mother telling her many reasons why she must always listen to her mother. Her mother told Rose that she did not have enough wood and this was why she bent too easily and listened to others rather than to her mother. Rose admits to herself that she always listened to others instead of her mother.

Rose becomes distressed when Ted says he wants a divorce. One essayist writes, "Whereas the major problem for the older generation had been the struggle against fate, the younger generation perceives their essential difficulty to involve the making of choices. The problem, as Rose Hsu Jordan defines it, is that America offers too many choices, 'so much to think about, so much to decide. Each decision meant a turn in another direction.'"[1] In short, while Chinese culture seems too strict to the daughters, a more open and varied culture poses a new set of difficulties.

Overwhelmed by her confusion about her divorce, Rose stays in bed for days, ignoring the world. At one point she gets a phone call from her mother. Rose tells her mother that she does not want to hear her say she should work on fixing her marriage. In an essay on the novel, one critic explains: "The Chinese way consists of not expressing one's desires, not speaking up, and not making choices. . . . Indeed, in China people had no choice. Since they could not speak up, they were forced to accept whatever fate befell them."[2] Yet An-mei does not advise in the way that her daughter expects. Instead of telling Rose to stay in her marriage, she says she should speak up to her husband. An-mei is not so conservative as to believe all Chinese ways are right. She saw the horrible life her own mother lived and how she was driven to suicide. An-mei feels that her daughter should not have to swallow her desires, she should speak up and be able to make choices.

Rose now feels that her mother is on her side. Rose's confusion finally abates when she stands up to her husband. She tells her husband that her lawyer will draw up papers with divorce terms and that she wants to keep the house.

CHAPTER 9

The Joy Luck Club and Tan's Other Works

The Joy Luck Club is one of the most well-known and appreciated works by a contemporary Asian-American author. It is even more outstanding because it was Tan's first published book. While Tan's parents had envisioned their daughter becoming a surgeon, Tan says she had experiences and a history that made it logical to become a writer instead. For instance, while Tan was distressed at each of her family's relocations, she realized later how these moves helped fine-tune her writing skills:

> By the time I graduated from high school, I had attended eleven schools. I had learned to lose friends, to remain the

loner until I finally found new ones. Each time I started

at a school, I had to sit back quietly for the first month

or so and observe. . . . I understood that I had to be a

chameleon to survive, that I should fit in quietly,

and watch.

In hindsight, I see that this was excellent training for a

budding writer. It sharpened my skills of observation. It

deepened my sense of alienation. . . .[1]

Aside from this personal experience, Tan found out later in life that her family has its own history of storytelling. One grandfather was an editor and another grandfather was a minister, who, of course, had to write sermons for his job. Tan's father was also a minister who had to write sermons, and her mother was constantly telling stories of her life in China.

Indeed, *The Joy Luck Club* is made up of sixteen short stories, some of which are based on the storytelling of Tan's own mother.

Tan writes of her mother:

When she remembered an event from her past, especially a traumatic one, it was as though she had boarded a time machine and had been transported to the moment she was remembering. . . .

. . . [T]o me, her memories were gifts. . . . "Can you imagine?" my mother would say to me, as she told her story. She would repeat this question often, making me work harder to imagine it.[2]

Not only does Tan base some of *The Joy Luck Club* on her mother's stories, but Tan also tells her stories in similarly vivid detail and with striking metaphors. At times she transports us to a time in China, foreign to most of today's American readers. Her work focuses on how Asian-American daughters grow up in America. Seemingly, they want to be Americans and out of the grip of their meddlesome, critical, and old-fashioned mothers. Yet Tan skillfully weaves her stories so that slowly the perspective changes. Most pointedly, June whose mother has died, reconnects with her through the mother's friends and other daughters. As readers progress through the work, they too, start to see the mothers differently, as well as the daughters.

After so much success with her first book, Tan felt pressured about how she could produce another book as good or better. Working on her second book, she made numerous false starts and then settled on the story of *The Kitchen God's Wife*.

The Joy Luck Club focused on four different relationships, but here the focus is on only one mother and daughter. Also, while the characters in *The Joy Luck Club* each had the same opportunity to tell their stories, here most of the book is told through the mother only.

As in her first book, Tan explores the mother-daughter relationship, in this case one that is not doing very well. Yet the relationship is revitalized when the mother tells her daughter the story of her past in China: a story she had thought best to keep to herself so she could save her daughter from its horror and pain. The daughter, too, had been keeping her own secret in the belief that it would be too painful to her mother. The daughter recognizes she must tell her secret to her mother and that her secret is small compared to what her mother has to tell. In this book, like Tan's first, we again see the dangers of patriarchal societies and the influence of Chinese culture, superstitions, and myths.

Tan's 1992 book, *The Moon Lady*, is a children's book, a new venue for Tan. The book actually retells a story from *The Joy Luck Club* in a way that is enjoyable to children. Children are taken to the world of China and are reminded to be careful about their wishes, and that they need to be responsible.

In 1993, *The Joy Luck Club* was released as a film. Tan wrote the screenplay with Ronald Bass (who wrote *Rain Man*), and Wayne Wang directed it. Tan was also one of the film's producers and appeared in it briefly. With no experience in filmmaking, Tan wondered how she would manage during the process: "Why would any writer in her right mind ever consider making a movie instead? That's like going from being a monk or a nun to serving as a camp counselor for hundreds of problem children."[3] Yet Tan found the process not nearly as bad as she had feared. She was happy that collaborating meant discussions and that they were followed by time to write on her own. She was also determined to have creative control and was most pleased when Disney gave her just that.

After this, Tan published another children's book, *The Chinese Siamese Cat*, which inspired a series on PBS television called *Sagwa*. In this book, children read a tale through a cat's point of view. The cats in the story see the results of the oppressive edicts of the ruler yet feel they can do nothing about them. However, one cat shows that taking a risk can produce positive results.

With *The Hundred Secret Senses*, published in 1995, Tan again ventured into new territory, delving into the world of the supernatural and merging it with reality, again receiving mostly favorable reviews. In this novel, unlike her others,

Tan uses only one character as the narrator. This narrator also retells stories of another character, giving us a secondhand account. Once again, Tan has her readers see her characters a certain way and then manages to change that perspective.

In this case, have a young woman (the narrator) and an older Chinese half sister who is a meddler (not unlike the daughters and their mothers in *The Joy Luck Club* initially appear). The Chinese half sister is said to be able to communicate with the dead and to have other extraordinary powers. In between Chinese tales, readers learn of the younger woman's faltering marriage. Yet this woman's perspective and her marriage change for the better when the woman, her husband, and her half sister visit China. There, the woman starts to believe she may have lived there in a former life, just as her half sister has said. Inexplicably, the Chinese half sister disappears, and the couple that has not been able to conceive, has a child.

Themes that Tan examines in her earlier titles are also explored in *The Bonesetter's*

Daughter, published in 2001. Tan was writing the book as her mother was getting sicker from Alzheimer's disease. When her mother died and her good friend and editor died two weeks later, Tan took the manuscript and revamped it. "The writing was a way to go back and reflect. I think when anyone goes through the loss of another person, it's hard to talk about it and yet you need to talk about it," she later said in an interview. "When they died two weeks apart, I almost threw the book away because it seemed so meaningless compared to what I'd gone through."[4]

In the novel, the mother is also losing her memory. But she has written many pages and has given them to her daughter. The daughter eventually asks someone to translate these for her. The novel is broken into three sections, two parts told from the daughter's perspective, although written in the third person, and a middle section that is the translation of the mother's story. During the mother's story, we learn not only her secrets but also secrets her mother, in turn, had kept from her. As in other Tan novels, we see what wedges have been between mothers and daughters as well as what makes them similar. We see difficulties due to generational differences and cultural differences. There is added poignancy as the mother loses her faculties and both mother and daughter must adjust.

Adjustment is also discussed in Tan's *The Opposite of Fate: A Book of Musings*, a collection of short pieces Tan published in 2003. While some of the ideas that run through her novels appear here, Tan speaks directly to her audience rather than through a fictional narrator. We learn about her own life and tragedies, about how disturbing it really was to live with her own mother, about how it feels to be a well-known author, and about her anxieties. But we also see Tan's humor, optimism, humility, strength, determination, and ability to love the mother who was so difficult. In an interview, Tan revealed part of that mixed response to her mother, "What I do sense is the loss of the person who worried the most for me. I don't know how to explain it . . . it was so irritating for so many years that she worried to the point of my aggravation and now that she's gone I feel that no one else in the world will worry as much about me. It makes me feel more vulnerable."[5]

In 2005, Tan went in a different direction with her work. Some of her same concerns about fate, reality, and understanding ourselves appeared in her new novel, yet the deep mother-daughter issue that had been so prevalent in many of her books was no longer the central concern. This more lighthearted novel, *Saving Fish from Drowning*, tells of Americans visiting Burma and how they are held by a tribe who believes the group's young teenager is a reincarnated god who will save the tribe from its enemy. Here, the narrator is the character who was to be the group's tour guide, but has died. Readers also learn the thoughts of the other characters and see how the group manages in this foreign land.

While Tan's first work remains her most

popular, the fact that so many of her other books were favorably received is to her credit. Her most recent novel shows her willingness to delve into something outside her usual realm. She was fortunate to work for years with an editor who pushed her to do her best. As Tan writes, "she also prodded me to go deeper, to be more generous in the story I had to tell, to not hold back. . . ."[6]

CHAPTER 10

The Joy Luck Club in Context

Asian-American literature, for the most part, became an acknowledged branch of literature due to the Asian-American movement of the 1960s and 1970s. This movement was an outgrowth of civil rights activism in the United States. Specifically, Asian-American activists focused on improvements in housing, health care, education, and employment. Additionally, during this time student activists fought for inclusion of Asian-American history as part of a college education.

The actual term *Asian American* was created by such activists. Over time, however, the term has taken on various definitions. For instance, the term initially seemed to imply a limited group, those from China and Japan. Other groups, such as Filipinos and South Asians, were concerned that the term sounded like it did not include them. Similarly, the term *Asian-American literature* has been scrutinized for an array of reasons: whether it applies to people with some Asian origin mixed with other ancestry; whether it applies to literature written by someone who is both Asian and American but not necessarily writing about that experience; etc. As with terminology that does not have a very long history, these definitions will probably continue to be reviewed and altered. Currently, the terminology includes rather wide definitions and applies to a range of people and literature.

In examining Chinese-American literature and how *The Joy Luck Club* fits in such a tradition, it is helpful to go back further than the 1960s and 1970s. For example, certainly people of Chinese ancestry were in the United States before the 1960s and 1970s, so why did it take so long for their literature to be acknowledged? A large

JUST GUESTS

Some of the earliest Chinese immigrants came to the United States to work in mining during the California gold rush. Later, in the 1860s, they were brought in to work on the transcontinental railroad. Many Americans were

prejudiced against them, seeing them not as a new group that could add to the diversity and talent of the country but as a group that should only come to work. These men should make money in the United States and then return to their families in China, some Americans thought.

In their racist eyes, these men were less than Caucasian immigrants. As a result, laws were passed to keep the Chinese from gaining any further access to an American way of life. The first of several Chinese Exclusion Acts was passed in 1882. Under the laws, Chinese women could not immigrate to the United States to be with their husbands, Chinese men who had worked in the United States and gone home were not certain they would be allowed back into the United States, and white women who married Chinese men lost their

citizenship. It was not until 1943 that such restrictions were repealed.

America's perception toward Asians was altered with World War II. For many Americans, the Japanese were seen as enemies and the Chinese were seen as loyal to the United States, since they were suffering at the hands of the Japanese as well. In 1943, the 1882 Chinese Exclusion Act was repealed but the number of Chinese women in the United States still lagged far behind the number of Chinese men for some time. Not until 1965 did additional legislation further loosen restrictions on immigration.

number of Chinese immigrants started arriving in the United States during the California gold rush of 1848. In addition to working in the mines, Chinese men were also brought to this country to work on the railroad. American citizens viewed these men as visitors to this country who were not looking to stay but only to make money that they could take back to their native lands. Indeed, a series of laws were passed to keep Chinese immigrants from becoming citizens and gaining rights.

At the time, since most of the Chinese in America were laborers and working an excessive number of hours, they were not focused on producing literature. It is not surprising, then, that two of the first successful writers in the Chinese-American tradition were women, the sisters Edith Maude Eaton and Winnifred Eaton. Their father was English, and their mother was Chinese. While the daughters were born in England, they moved to the United States as adults and began writing under Asian pseudonyms, with Edith's first work appearing in the

1880s. Edith wrote many short stories, focusing on the racism facing Chinese immigrants to North America, as well as focusing on the prejudice against other groups. She created sympathetic but realistic characters that, because of their mixed ethnicity, are abandoned by people from both heritages.

Edith used a Chinese pseudonym while Winnifred used a Japanese name. At the time, many Americans were against the Chinese but had some respect for the Japanese. Winnifred's writings made no attempt to point out prejudices or right wrongs but instead reinforced them. She wrote appealing romances with pleasant Japanese women saved by white men in interesting foreign locales. Her career took off.

PSEUDONYM
A name that is used by a person but that is not that person's real name; often used on published works.

For the most part, though, Chinese Americans in the late 1800s and early 1900s were writing autobiographies that responded to racism by attempting to explain Chinese culture and customs. The rationale was that if the Chinese were not seen as so foreign, they would be accepted. A slight change can be seen in the works of some second-generation Chinese-American authors, who more realistically portrayed the difficulty of growing up a product of two very different cultures. Still, many of these authors continued to reinforce America's narrow perspective and focused only on lives of the upper class and highly educated Chinese. In the mid-1940s, well-received authors were Pardee Lowe (*Father and Glorious Descendant*, 1943) and Jade Snow Wong (*Fifth Chinese Daughter*, 1945 and 1950). Few Asian-American works appeared for the next few decades.

A notable change occurred in 1961 with the publication of Louis Chu's novel *Eat a Bowl of Tea*. Some experts see the title as the beginning of realism in Asian-American writing. Not only does Chu focus on the typical Asian American in the United States rather than those in the upper rung, but he also explores the dark side of life for these inhabitants. The novel is set in 1947 and shows the trying adjustments the Chinese Americans struggle through as well as the difficulties confronting them because of racism and the traditionally patriarchal Chinese society.

As mentioned previously, the 1970s witnessed the Asian-American movement. Like the civil rights movement and the women's liberation movement, the Asian-American movement saw a questioning of the constraints on its people, as well as a drive to do something about them. As an outgrowth of this radicalism, Chinese-American literature also became more radical. The author Frank Chin, for example, wrote of the Chinese American who belongs not to the traditional Chinese culture, nor to the pervasive, individualistic American culture that surrounds him and that has rejected him. Rather, he has his own culture.

Chin was the first Chinese American to have a play produced on the New York stage. When *The Chickencoop Chinaman* was first performed in 1972, it received mixed reviews, even from such liberal publications as *The New York Times* and *The Village Voice*. "It was an outpouring of bitterness and hatred mouthed through lengthy monologue after monologue," wrote Betty Lee Sung in *East/West*.[1] Chin is also known for being an editor of one of the best-known anthologies of Asian-American literature, published in 1974 and revised and expanded in 1991. Other anthologies of Asian-American writing published in the 1970s also brought such literature into view.

Additionally, a group called the Combined Asian Resources Project helped give a voice to Asian-American literature. The group helped get Asian-American works published and performed, even some texts that had been out of print; produced materials about their authors; and sponsored conferences where Asian-American texts were discussed.

Maxine Hong Kingston became one of the most famous Chinese-American women authors during this time, due to her publication of *The*

Woman Warrior in 1976 and *China Men* in 1980. Both won the National Book Critic's Circle Award. The American public also enthusiastically took notice. Kingston's texts explore not only Chinese-American identity, but also comment on the complex interaction of genders, cultures, and classes. Kingston's writing has gotten criticism from a few, people of Asian descent for, among other reasons, what they call her "giving in to pleasing whites." Some critics, such as Chin and his fellow

DRIVEN TO DESPERATION

In *The Joy Luck Club*, An-mei watched her mother commit suicide, driven to desperation because of her lowly status as concubine. Ying-ying, when her husband left her and she found out how much he had been cheating on her, considered drowning herself. While these women are fictional characters, Amy Tan based them and their experiences on reality. Women in traditional Chinese culture have low status and are taught to be submissive; some, unfortunately, suffer to such a degree that they feel they have no alternatives but death.

Tan's own mother often threatened to commit suicide, and Tan and her brother were highly disturbed, upset, and fearful because of this. Both sister and brother as adults realized they inherited some of their mother's rage and self-destructive urge. In *The Opposite of Fate*, published in 2003, Tan reported on findings about Chinese women committing suicide: "I recently learned that in China today, a third of all deaths among women in rural areas are suicides. Nationwide, more than two million Chinese women each year attempt suicide, and 300,000 succeed. And in contrast to any other country, more women than men in China kill themselves. I pondered this. Conditions for women in China have changed for the better in the last hundred years, and life in the country-side may not be egalitarian, but is it really so bad . . . ?"[2]

anthology editors, criticized Kingston and others, including Amy Tan. For the most part, though, these critics are in the minority.

In fact, when one considers Chinese-American women writers in the context of Chinese culture, such women are true pioneers:

> In her groundbreaking study on women writers of Chinese ancestry, Between Worlds, Amy Ling observes that . . . [b]ecause of the high value placed on feminine modesty and reticence in Chinese culture . . . a woman of Chinese ancestry who wants to publish in the United States "must be something of a rebel, for writing, an act of rebellion and self-assertion, runs counter to Confucian training. Also she has to possess two basic character traits: an indomitable will and an unshakeable self-confidence."[3]

According to Ling, then, Tan and others are rebels just for writing, regardless of what that writing says. For Tan—like Kingston and many others writing mostly in the 1970s and after— the alienation of not belonging to either the

American or Chinese culture remains key. Additionally, in *The Joy Luck Club*, Tan, like some other authors, focuses on mother-daughter relationships and differences between generations as well as between past and present.

In Tan's case, *The Joy Luck Club* had broad and popular appeal. Critics have compared her writing not only to that of other Chinese Americans but to that of James Joyce and William Faulkner. Rather than following a linear narrative, Tan experiments in *The Joy Luck Club* with other methods, interweaving stories from multiple characters, and including dreams, versions of myths, and oral storytelling. Indeed, Tan herself has stated that she does not want her work to be examined as a work of minority literature. Anyone who has been in a family can relate to the work.

CHRONOLOGY

1952 Amy Tan is born on February 19 in Oakland, California, the second of three children, to Daisy Tu Ching Tan and John Yuehhan Tan.

1972 Earns bachelor's degree in English and linguistics at San Jose State University.

1973 Earns master's degree in linguistics.

1974 Marries Louis M. DeMattei, a tax attorney, in April 1974. Begins work on doctorate at University of California, Berkeley.

1976 Leaves Berkeley and takes position as language-development specialist for disabled children.

1981 Leaves position to become reporter for medical journal, eventually becoming managing editor and then associate publisher.

1983 Becomes freelance technical writer.

1987 Travels to China with her mother and husband to meet two of her three half sisters for the first time.

1989 Publishes *The Joy Luck Club*, a *New York Times* hardcover best-seller for nine months and a finalist for the National Book Award and the National Book Critics Circle Award.

1991 Publishes *The Kitchen God's Wife*.

1992 Publishes *The Moon Lady*, a children's book.

1993 Film version of *The Joy Luck Club* is released; created in collaboration with the screenwriter Ronald Bass.

1994 Publishes the children's book *The Chinese Siamese Cat*.

1995 Publishes *The Hundred Secret Senses*.

2001 Publishes *The Bonesetter's Daughter*.

2003 Publishes a collection of essays, *The Opposite of Fate: A Book of Musings*.

2005 Publishes *Saving Fish from Drowning*.

Chapter 1. Biography

1. "Interview: Amy Tan, Best-Selling Novelist," June 28, 1996, Sun Valley, Idaho, July 17, 2006, Academy of Achievement, <http://www.achievement.org/autodoc/ page/tan0int-1> (January 11, 2007).

2. Ibid.

Chapter 3. Themes

1. Catherine Romagnolo, "Narrative Beginnings in Amy Tan's *The Joy Luck Club*: A Feminist Study," *Studies in the Novel*, vol. 35, March 22, 2003.

2. Victoria Chen, "Chinese American Women, Language, and Moving Subjectivity," *Women and Language*, vol. 18, no. 1, Spring 1995.

3. Amy Tan, *The Joy Luck Club* (New York: Ballantine Books, 1989), p. 124.

4. Ibid., p. 91.

5. Ibid., p. 82.

6. Ibid., p. 3.

Chapter 4. Literary Devices

1. Wendy Ho, "Teaching Amy Tan's *The Joy Luck Club*," *Amy Tan's* The Joy Luck Club, Harold Bloom, editor (Philadelphia: Chelsea House Publishers, 2003), p. 150.

2. Sau-Ling Cynthia Wong, "'Sugar Sisterhood': Situating the Amy Tan Phenomenon," *Amy Tan's* The Joy Luck Club, Harold Bloom, editor (Philadelphia: Chelsea House Publishers, 2003), p. 91.

3. Amy Tan, *The Joy Luck Club* (New York: Ballantine Books, 1989), p. 8.

4. Ibid., p. 13.

Chapter 5. Suyuan Woo and Jing-mei "June" Woo

1. Gloria Shen, "Storytelling in Amy Tan's *The Joy Luck Club*," *Amy Tan's* The Joy Luck Club, Harold Bloom, editor (Philadelphia: Chelsea House Publishers, 2003), p. 118.

2. Victoria Chen, "Chinese American Women, Language, and Moving Subjectivity," *Women and Language*, vol. 18, no. 1, Spring 1995.

3. Amy Tan, *The Joy Luck Club* (New York: Ballantine Books, 1989), p. 143.

Chapter 6. Lindo Jong and Waverly Jong

1. Walter Shear, "Generational Differences and the Diaspora in *The Joy Luck Club*," *CRITIQUE: Studies in Contemporary Fiction*, vol. 34, no. 3, Spring 1993.

2. Ibid.

Chapter 7. Ying-ying St. Clair and Lena St. Clair

1. Walter Shear, "Generational Differences and the Diaspora in *The Joy Luck Club*," *CRITIQUE: Studies in Contemporary Fiction*, vol. 34, no. 3, Spring 1993.

2. Ibid.

Chapter 8. An-mei Hsu and Rose Hsu Jordan

1. Walter Shear, "Generational Differences and the Diaspora in *The Joy Luck Club*," *CRITIQUE: Studies in Contemporary Fiction*, vol. 34, no. 3, Spring 1993.

2. Gloria Shen, "Storytelling in Amy Tan's *The Joy Luck Club*," *Amy Tan's* The Joy Luck Club, Harold Bloom, editor (Philadelphia: Chelsea House Publishers, 2003), p. 117.

Chapter 9. *The Joy Luck Club* and Tan's Other Works

1. Amy Tan, *The Opposite of Fate* (New York: G.P. Putnam's Sons, 2003), p. 22.

2. Ibid., p. 81.

3. "Interview, March 2001," *Bookreporter.com*, <http://www.bookreporter.com/authors /au-tan-amy.asp> (January 15, 2007).

4. Tan, p. 178.

5. "Interview, March 2001."

6. Tan, p. 63.

Chapter 10. *The Joy Luck Club* in Context

1. Quoted in Deborah L. Madsen, *Chinese American Writers* (Farmington Hills, Mich.: Gale Group, 2001), pp. 110–111.

2. Amy Tan, *The Opposite of Fate* (New York: G.P. Putnam's Sons, 2003), p. 80.

3. Jeanne Rosier Smith, "Maxine Hong Kingston's Transformational Trickster Texts," *Asian-American Writers*, Harold Bloom, editor (Philadelphia: Chelsea House, 1999), p. 201.

capitalism—An economic system wherein business takes place in an open, competitive market.

Confucian—Referring to the teachings of Confucius, a famous Chinese philosopher (551 to 479 b.c.e) who emphasized self-control, adherence to a social chain of command, and social and political order.

empathize—To understand someone's feelings, thoughts, and experiences.

imperialism—A country's act of ruling or influencing other countries or lands.

irony—The incongruity of an expected situation and the actual situation. In language, irony is the deliberate use of words to contrast an apparent meaning with the words' intended meaning (which are usually the complete opposite of each other).

mahjong—A game of 144 small tiles; it originated in China and usually involves four players who draw and discard tiles until one player gets a winning hand.

patriarchy—A culture where men have the most power.

pseudonym—A name that is used by a person but that is not that person's real name; often used on published works.

prodigy—Someone with an outstanding talent that appears when the person is quite young.

reincarnate—To be born again in a different body.

South Asian—A person from the countries of Bangladesh, Bhutan, India, the Maldives, Nepal, Pakistan, or Sri Lanka.

symbol—Something that stands for, represents, or suggests another thing.

MAJOR WORKS
OF AMY TAN

FURTHER READING

Books

Amy Tan's The Joy Luck Club. Harold Bloom, ed. Broomall, Pa.: Chelsea House, 2002.

Hoobler, Dorothy and Thomas Hoobler. *The Chinese-American Family Album*. New York: Oxford University Press, 1998.

Ishizuka, Kathy. *Asian American Authors*. Berkeley Heights, N.J.: Enslow Publishers, Inc., 2000.

Kramer, Barbara. *Amy Tan: Author of* The Joy Luck Club. Berkeley Heights, N.J.: Enslow Publishers, Inc., 1996.

Internet Addresses

Amy Tan Overview
http://academic.brooklyn.cuny.edu/english/melani/cs6/tan.html

***The Joy Luck Club* Book Notes**
http://www.bookrags.com/notes/jlc/

***The Joy Luck Club* Resource Guide**
http://www.duluth.lib.mn.us/Programs/JoyLuckClub/ResourceGuide.html

INDEX